TABLE OF CONTENTS

INTRODUCTION

Real estate is referred to as the land as well as any permanent, whether natural or man-made, structures or improvements related to the property, such as a house.

One type of real property is real estate. It contrasts from personal property, such as cars, yachts, jewels, furniture, and farm equipment, which is not permanently affixed to the land.
Real estate is something permanently affixed to or constructed on land, whether it be created naturally or artificially.
Real estate may be divided into five primary categories: residential, commercial, industrial, raw land, and special use.
Buying a house, a rental property, or land is a real estate investment.
Real estate investments are two options for indirect real estate investing.
There are differences between land, real estate, and real property, while they are frequently used interchangeably.

Land includes the plants, minerals, and water that are present on the earth's surface up to its center and above it in the upper atmosphere. The immobility, invulnerability, and distinctiveness of land, where each parcel of land differs regionally, are some of its physical properties.
Real estate includes the land as well as any enduring human constructions, including homes and other structures. An improvement is any addition to or alteration to the land that raises or lowers the property's value.

After land has been upgraded, the sum of the labor and capital utilized to construct the improvement will constitute a substantial fixed investment. Even though a structure can be demolished, upgrades to the plumbing, electrical, water, and sewer systems are frequently long-lasting.
Real property consists of the land, its improvements, as well as the underlying ownership and usage rights.

WHAT KINDS OF REAL ESTATE ARE THERE?

Any property used for residential purposes is considered residential real estate. Single-family homes, condominiums, cooperatives, duplexes, townhouses, and multifamily buildings are a few examples.

Commercial Real Estate includes any property used only for commercial activities, including office buildings, retail malls, restaurants, hotels, petrol stations, grocery shops, theaters, hospitals, and office buildings.
Industrial Real Estate: Any property utilized for production, distribution, storage, manufacturing.
Land: This category includes undeveloped real estate, open space, and agricultural grounds including farms, orchards, ranches, and wooded areas.
Special purpose: Real estate that is utilized by the general public, such as cemeteries, government structures, libraries, parks, and schools.
Housing starts, or the number of new residential building projects in any given month, as reported by the U.S. Census Bureau, is an important economic indicator. Real estate is a crucial economic engine in the U.S and every other part of the world. For single-family houses, residences with 2-4 units, and multifamily structures with five units or more, such as apartment buildings, the report provides statistics on construction permits, housing starts, and housing completions.
A piece of ground and anything that is affixed to it permanently are considered real property. Real estate owners are entitled to full ownership privileges, including the freedom to use, own, sell, and lease their property.

Real estate can be categorized as residential, commercial, agricultural, industrial, or special purpose depending on its general usage. Knowing what rights you have and do not have in the property is necessary to determine if you have the right to sell your house.
Real estate is referred to as land that is on, above, or below the surface of the ground, as well as any structures that are firmly affixed to it, whether they be man-made or natural.
Real estate and real property are identical in everyday usage.
All items that don't fall within the real property definition are referred to as personal property, including clothing, automobiles, and furniture.
Starting with land and real estate is helpful in understanding how real property is defined. Land is anything that is permanently attached by nature (or at least attached for the foreseeable future), such as stones, trees, and water. Land extends upward to infinity and below to the earth's center.
"Estate in land" refers to the size and nature of a person's stake in real estate. The two main categories of estates in land are freehold estates and non-freehold estates.

REAL ESTATE INVESTMENT
101

Housing is usually the first thing that springs to mind when you consider investing in real estate. Real estate investors, of course, have a wide range of other choices for investments, and they are not limited to real estate.

Over the past 50 years or more, real estate has gained popularity as a means of investment. Here are some of the best alternatives available to individual investors, along with some motivations for doing so.

A well-diversified portfolio should at least include real estate, which is regarded as a separate asset class.

Investing in real estate and becoming a landlord is one of the best methods for investors to profit.

Flippers aim to purchase real estate that is undervalued, improve it, and resell it for a profit.

Without the need to own, manage, or finance real estate, real estate investment trusts, offer indirect real estate exposure.

For good reason, real estate has long been regarded as a wise investment. Prior to 2007, historical housing statistics gave the impression that prices might rise endlessly. Between 1963 and 2007—the year the Great Recession began—the average sale price of homes in the U.S. rose annually with few exceptions. At the start of the COVID-19 epidemic in the spring of 2020, home prices did experience a little decline. Home values, however, increased quickly and reached all-time highs by 2022 as vaccinations were introduced and pandemic fears subsided.

You become a landlord if you invest in rental homes, so you should think about whether you'll feel at home in that position. You will be in charge of things like finding renters, keeping the property maintained, paying the mortgage, insurance, and property taxes, as well as handling any issues that arise.

Being a landlord requires a lot of time and effort, unless you employ a property manager to take care of the technicalities. Taking care of the property and the renters may be a 24/7 job, and it's not always enjoyable, depending on your circumstances. However, the likelihood of experiencing significant issues can be reduced if you chose your homes and renters properly.

Rent is one method that landlords can generate income.

The location of the property will determine how much rent you may charge. Even yet, choosing the optimum rent may be challenging since if you ask for too much, you'll lose renters, and if you ask for too little, you'll lose money. One popular tactic is to demand rent that is sufficient to pay costs until the mortgage has been paid, at which time the majority of the rent becomes profit.

The other main source of income for landlords is appreciation.

If the value of your property rises, you might be able to sell it for a profit (when the time is right) or take out a loan against the equity to fund your subsequent investment. There are no assurances, even if real estate does frequently increase in value.

This is especially true when the real estate market is experiencing high levels of volatility, most notably during the COVID-19 epidemic. The United States' median real estate prices increased by an astounding 38% between February 2020 and March 2022. Many people have begun to question if prices are about to drop owing to the extraordinary surge.

Real estate flippers are a whole different breed from buy-and-rent landlords, just like day traders are miles apart from buy-and-hold investors. Flippers purchase homes with the goal to retain them for a little time—typically no more than three to four months—and then rapidly flip them for a profit.

TO FLIP A PROPERTY, THERE ARE TWO MAIN METHODS:

Update and repair. With this strategy, you purchase a home that you believe will appreciate in value after some renovations and modifications. Ideally, you finish the project as soon as possible and then sell it for more money than you originally invested (including the renovations).

Keep and sell again. Flipping operates differently in this case. You buy in a quickly growing area rather than purchasing a house and renovating it rises the market value, invest for a few months, and then make money off of the sale.

You incur the danger of not being able to sell the home for a price that will result in a profit with any form of flipping. This can be difficult since flippers typically don't retain enough cash on hand to cover long-term mortgage payments on homes. However, if done correctly, flipping may be a profitable method to invest in real estate.

REITs When a company (or trust) is established with the purpose of using investor funds to buy, manage, and resell properties that generate income, a real estate investment trust (REIT) is formed. Similar to stocks and exchange-traded funds, REITs may be purchased and sold on major exchanges (ETFs).

90% of the company's taxable income must be distributed to shareholders as dividends in order for it to be considered a REIT. By doing this, REITs avoid paying corporate income tax, as opposed to a traditional business, which would pay tax on its profits and reduce the returns it can give shareholders.

REITs are suitable for investors who desire consistent income, much like normal dividend-paying securities, albeit they also provide the chance for gain. REITs make a range of property investments.

Real Estate Investment groups, resemble mini-mutual funds for rental properties. A real estate investment group can be the answer for you if you want to own a rental property but don't want the headache of being a landlord.

A business will acquire or construct a collection of structures, frequently apartments, and then permit investors to acquire those structures directly from the business. Self-contained dwelling units may be owned by a single investor in one or more buildings. However, the organization that runs the investment group administers every property and handles maintenance, advertising, and tenant placement. The business retains a portion of the monthly rent in return for this management.
Investment groups come in several forms. The investor is named on the lease in the regular version, and all of the units share a percentage of the rent to protect against sporadic vacancies. This implies that even if your apartment is vacant, you will still get enough to cover the mortgage.

An investment group's quality is totally dependent on the firm that provides it. Theoretically, it is a secure method to start investing in real estate, but organizations may impose the same excessive fees that plague the mutual fund sector. Research is essential for all investments.

Housing starts are closely monitored by analysts and investors since the data can give a broad indication of the trajectory of the economy. Additionally, the sorts of new home starts might reveal information about the state of the economy.
Home ownership, rental or investment homes, and house flipping are some of the most popular real estate investment strategies. Real estate wholesalers are one form of real estate investor that contracts a house with a seller before locating a buyer. Wholesalers of real estate typically locate and acquire bankrupt properties without making any improvements or modifications.

Real estate investments provide returns through increase in property value as well as rent or lease income. The year-end 2021 U.S. house sales report from ATTOM, which manages the country's leading property database, reveals that home sellers countrywide realized a profit of $94,092, a 45.3%return on investment, up 45% from $64,931 in 2020 and up 71% from $55,000 two years ago.
Real estate investment is a method that may be both rewarding and profitable. Prospective real estate owners can utilize leverage to purchase a property, unlike stock and bond investors, by paying a percentage of the entire cost up front and then paying off the remainder, plus interest, over time.

Although a 20% to 25% down payment is often required for a standard mortgage, in rare circumstances, a 5% down payment is all that is needed to buy the entire home. Both real estate flippers and landlords are empowered by the ability to assume possession of the asset as soon as the paperwork is signed and can, in turn, take out second mortgages on their homes to pay down payments on more properties. Here are the top five ways investors may profit.

Aspiring real estate owners can purchase a home by employing leverage, making a down payment equal to a percentage of the entire price, and paying off the remaining balance over time.

Being a landlord of a rental property is one of the main ways that real estate investors may generate money.

Flippers, who purchase undervalued real estate, renovate it, and then sell it, may also make money.

A more passive method of making money in real estate is through real estate investment groups.

Self-contained living units may be owned by a single investor in one or more units, but the business managing the investment group oversees all of the units, taking care of upkeep, advertising vacancies, and conducting tenant interviews. The business receives a portion of the monthly fee in return for performing these management duties.

A typical real estate investment group lease is in the name of the investor, and the rent for each unit is combined to protect against sporadic vacancies. This means that even if your unit is vacant, you will still make some money. There should be enough to pay expenses, so long as the vacancy rate for the pooled apartments doesn't surge too high.

When easterners crossed this huge nation in search of opportunity in the recently opened regions during the Wild West era, they were sometimes referred to as "tenderfoots."

This wasn't a flattering phrase, but it was a good one. The easterners were dressed in "city" footwear that was not made to resist the challenges of the western landscape. Their attire wasn't composed of durable fabric like denim, and their hats didn't have large brims to shield them from the sun.

These new Westerners had no notion how to take care of themselves, and they had no concept how to avoid risks because they didn't know where or what they were. If you are just starting to think about investing in Real estate, you're a greenhorn who needs some guidance to keep from losing your shirt... along with your jeans, hat, and boots most likely.

In order to invest in real estate, you must first decide on your plan. Do you want to buy a house, make improvements to it, and then sell it right away, or do you want to buy a house, hang onto it, and wait for the market to recover? Do you wish to manage tenants? You must have answers to each of these queries before making an investment in any real estate.

You'll need to develop the skills necessary to do your own property value research. It is unfair to take advantage of a real estate agent's time by asking them to show you several properties as you try to find a solid real estate investment.
There are several useful websites online in figuring out a property's true market worth. AVOID depending on tax values. Both their accuracy and dependability are lacking. Online, you may identify real estate agents you can deal with and read recommendations for them.

The next thing you require is a reputable broker who you can also work with once you have learnt how to evaluate properties on your own and have selected a real estate agent you can deal with. Request the names of three mortgage brokers from your real estate agent.

The next step is to research the interest rates and closing expenses associated with each option. (Consult your neighborhood bank or credit union as well.) Duplicates of your select a sample property for each broker to perform hard calculations on, and order three credit reports.

You are now prepared to make your first investment. To put a contract on, you want to pick the house with the lowest price in the finest area.
Consider that the least expensive two-bedroom home in Fort Wayne's nicest neighborhood costs $100,000, while the next-cheapest, identical property is offered for $140,000. If you purchase the house for $100,000, you may increase the price the next day to $130,000 and make a tidy little profit.

Let's now discuss how to seal the transaction. Display your pre-qualification letter from your lender to the seller first, then obtain your assessment and the necessary termite inspections. The ultimate closing takes roughly 30 days once you get your "ducks in a row," so to speak.

Please notice the following regarding any improvements or repairs you might wish to make to the property: To shut, you might want to consider a loan for purchases and renovations. With a Purchase and Renovate loan, the cost of construction is included in the loan, minimizing your out-of-pocket costs. A general contractor's estimate and architectural designs may be needed for this.

Let's return to the first task you had to do, which was to choose your approach. The moment has come for you to put your investment strategy for this real estate into action. If you acquired it with the intention of selling it when the market improved, all you have to do is wait.

It's time to begin your renovations if you purchased the property with the intention of selling it after renovations. However, if you purchased it with the intention of renting it out, it is now time to begin finding renters.

You see, since everything that follows depends on it, establishing a plan for making money from the acquisition of any piece of real estate must be your first choice.

Platforms for real estate investment are for those who wish to pool their money with others to participate in a larger commercial or residential purchase. The investment is done through real estate crowd funding sites, which are online real estate marketplaces. While less than what is needed to buy houses outright, this still requires funds for investment.

Online marketplaces bring together project financiers and developers of real estate. You may sometimes diversify your investments without spending a lot of money.

Can invest in single projects or portfolio of projects Geographic diversification.

Real estate investors may develop a comprehensive investment program by paying a very modest portion of a property's overall worth upfront, whether they use their assets to create rental income or to pass the time until the ideal selling opportunity presents itself. Real estate offers potential for profit regardless of how the market is performing overall, as with any investment.

Real estate investing may be profitable, but going it alone can be difficult and quite hazardous. Real estate investments may be profitable through partnerships, wholesale sales, and property management, to name a few strategies. In this very competitive industry, success also requires a little savviness.

A degree is not always necessary to succeed in real estate investment, while some colleges do provide basic courses and specialized programs that might be helpful to real estate investors. Top real estate investors frequently have similar traits, regardless of whether they have a degree or not.

A good strategy may help investors stay organized and on target because real estate investment can be challenging and complicated. The strategy would include projected costs and income inflows from rents, the number of units to buy, when to renovate or upgrade units, demographic changes, and anything else that could have an influence on your investment over time.

You might want to do some research on successful investors if you're interested in getting into the investment game and picking real estate as your main vehicle. Successful real estate investors have the expertise and know-how to successfully navigate the complex world of commercial and residential real estate. They have a strategy, the resources, and negotiation skills to turn real estate investment into a successful endeavor. The secret to becoming a profitable real estate investor is to focus on earning a profit, whether that profit comes from selling the property or comes from renting it out. There are certain "best-kept secrets" the experts utilize to do this that include more profitable projects.

Real estate investors are primarily concerned with capital and financing choices. When investing, you need to have a strategy in place as well as the resources necessary to handle any risks or surprises that may arise. Real estate may be very profitable, but there are hazards involved. Even if you have several potential properties and the funds to buy them, you can handle any issues that could arise far more skillfully. Make a financial strategy and budget, and stay within your bounds.

Think about all your options for financial gain as a real estate investor. You may purchase and sell commercial property, flip broken-down houses, and invest in rental properties properties and defer sales till they increase in value. Smart real estate investors consider all of their alternatives and do not restrict themselves to a single source of income or approach. It's a good idea to diversify in order to boost prospective rewards and thin out the risk.

WHY SHOULD I INVEST IN URBAN REAL ESTATE.

The urban area is the central portion of a city. The vast bulk of city dwellers reside here. The majority of the houses are clustered together in one location and split by narrow streets. Most cities' central business districts include a range of real estate, making them desirable as locations for rental homes.

Greater than average rates of more serious crimes are found in the inner city of most metropolitan locations. For a property owner who chooses a more secure neighborhood to invest in, there are some regions of the urban center that do not make ideal investment places due to gang violence and robberies.

If a threat to public safety exists, you should evacuate a place or remove a person from it. Owners of investment properties that fall behind on maintenance risk incurring costly code enforcement violations.

One of the problems that every property owner has to deal with is turnover. Generally speaking, homes within of cities may experience a greater churn rate, in part because of tenant job loss, incarceration, or short-term lease arrangements. High turnover can be reduced by using property management provided by a third-party organization to handle all tenant concerns.

In a metropolis, building regulations are frequently more stringent. City officials and management have the authority to shut down an apartment.
Real estate is one of the most well-liked, lucrative, and reliable investment options that may produce a significant profit return when done properly. The opportunity to create wealth, use equity as leverage, and safeguard your money from inflation are all benefits of real estate investing. Real estate investing also has incalculable advantages, such as enhancing communities, supplying homes, and creating networks. To succeed, be careful to pick the appropriate instruments and to be informed of the advantages and disadvantages of real estate investment.

An empty house will normally cost less to buy in an urban centre than it would in a more rural region. Supply and demand play a role in the lower pricing. When compared to the suburbs or more rural areas, the city has more dwellings crammed into a smaller space. Although long-term growth is essential for profitable urban rental properties, rent prices can occasionally be lower.

In metropolitan communities, a sizable portion of the residences that house families were constructed for expansion. More than two bedrooms are common in new homes, which appeal to bigger families. Multi-family housing is frequently seen inside the boundaries of cities. An ongoing stream of rental revenue is therefore provided.

Urban real estate is often not of interest to investors. This implies that individuals who are interested in investing in urban real estate have a lot of options. Let me offer you a few solid arguments for why you SHOULD invest in urban real estate as you will probably hear plenty of reasons why you shouldn't.

Let's start by talking about the cost of urban real estate. You can discover some true hidden gems in the urban real estate market if you maintain a "ear to the ground," so to speak. Of course, not every low price is a good deal, and as with every real estate transaction you ever make, you should be sure to do your research.

For a variety of reasons, very fantastic offers pop up in every real estate market. Because the house is located in an urban region, don't pass up those fantastic investment chances.

In addition, Section 8 renters must be taken into account. Buying real estate in a city has a number of clear benefits. In accordance with Section 8, wherein the government covers the whole 80% of the monthly rent, government-subsidized housing is a reality of the twenty-first century. 'Section 8 tenants' is a common term used to describe these renters. There is always a waiting list of tenants who want to move into YOUR metropolitan investment property, as is obvious.

You will now have a very great and reliable monthly income thanks to all of this. Occasionally, renters miss payments, but the government does issue checks on schedule and in full, which greatly reduces the headache of collecting rent.

Don't undervalue the possibility to renovate and flip real estate in metropolitan areas. Let's face it, then. The real estate market today might be much better. However, just because the market as a whole doesn't seem to be in the best of shape right now doesn't mean there aren't some fantastic repair and flip chances out there, especially in metropolitan areas. Selling an urban property with incentives included and, if it's a rental property, with a renter already residing there are the keys to generating a profit.

Don't forget about the United States of America's venerable government. In metropolitan locations, the government often finances initiatives to renovate whole neighborhoods. Local authorities receives money and frequently presents developers and property owners investing in these metropolitan communities with alluring incentives

.

Additionally, there are some very amazing interest rate deals that will allow you to keep your money safe and out of any danger. This results in a win-win-win scenario. The government is allowed to spend money, and they do it so well it seems. The locals in the area move into nicer houses, and you earn a tidy profit. Everyone benefits!

The clichéd real estate adage goes, "Location, location, and location are the only three things that count in real estate." That truly isn't always the case. Do you have any memories of playing the board game Monopoly as a child? Keep in mind those first tiny properties that were situated at the game's beginning?

They cost little. They were VERY affordable. Every participant in the game would have to land on it and pay you if you owned one of them right out of the gate, so to speak, since you could put a hotel up there practically quickly. It wasn't an expensive site, but it was a really excellent one. You might afford to make upgrades right away on it.

Consider investing in urban real estate the same way you would in Baltic or Mediterranean Avenues. It doesn't cost much to buy the property, and it doesn't cost much more to make renovations, so you can turn a profit fast and simply. It was a terrific Monopoly approach, and it's a smart urban real estate investing plan.

Investments in urban real estate satisfy every need for wise real estate investing.

In a city, the rental market is strong. There are many individuals who require housing, and that housing is frequently subsidized by the government.

Urban real estate is typically inexpensive and even available at incredibly alluring interest rates.

Market conditions are steady in metropolitan areas.
There is no boom-or-bust mindset. It is unlikely that demand will fall.

Urban real estate investing might be a wise choice, but you should always do your research before making a commitment

The Following Are The Main Benefits Of Investing In Urban Real Estate:

➢ Produce Wealth & Increase Equity

The strength of equity is the first of many benefits of real estate investing. When you own a home or other piece of property, its value always grows. You create equity when the mortgage is paid off and the value of the home rises. One of the easiest methods to build wealth is through equity, which is an asset that is a portion of your net worth. For instance, according to ALEX, homeowner equity increased by over threefold between 2011 and 2022.

You may produce cash flow and receive a return on your investment using a variety of choices using equity (ROI). You may make a sizable profit if you sell your house at the proper moment. As an alternative, you can leverage equity to grow your investment portfolio even more. You can purchase a rental property with equity from one property to increase the value of your equity portfolio and create monthly income.

➢ Trustworthy Long-Term Investment

Despite the real estate market's fluctuations, it is a reliable investment that never loses money. Real estate is less prone to market fluctuations or inflation than the stock market, which is a very volatile investment. Prices of properties do not alter right away as a result of capital contributions or Real estate is a secure and reliable long-term investment due of political unpredictability.

The graphs below illustrate the stock markets and the real estate market's historical fluctuations and expansion. Take note of the stock market graph's peaks and dips. The real estate graph climbs consistently upward over time, albeit having fewer ups and downs.
Real estate is also a tangible asset that can always be sold for a profit. Real estate ownership offers continual income and tax advantages as the value of the asset rises, which is advantageous to the investor. A cash-on-cash return is provided by renting the property, and a ROI is provided by living there and selling it again.

➢ Security Against Inflation

Real estate investors should not worry about inflation, unlike the majority of people. One of the most beneficial advantages of real estate investing in the present markets is that the impacts of inflation are rarely felt by properties. Real estate investments often increase in value alongside inflation rather than declining. In reality, the graph below

demonstrates how over the past three decades, property values have remained stable along with inflation.
As a real estate investor, your costs will rise in line with your income and property value. If you are a landlord, you may modify how much you charge for rent to preserve or even grow your income flow in response to inflation. When it comes time to raise the rent for your renters, be sure you are aware of all applicable rules and regulations, give the appropriate amount of notice, and compose a formal yet straightforward letter.

➢ Rental Property Income Is Passive

Real estate investing gives you the opportunity to create passive income. As previously noted, even if you don't make any improvements to the property, its value will increase automatically. Regardless of how many hours the owner spends maintaining the property or where they live, rental properties provide in a consistent monthly income for their owners. Investors have flexibility when they can profit from their real estate investments without having to commit a specific amount of time.

Obviously, investing in real estate requires a significant amount of labor on the part of the investor. Finding and evaluating an investment property, obtaining financing, preparing or maintaining the property, marketing the rental listing, and managing the property all need time and effort the occupants. But every step of the process may be easy and stress-free with the correct property management firm or tool.

➢ Provides Housing And Is Beneficial To The Community

There are unquantifiable advantages to investing in residential real estate, but most investors place a lot of emphasis on the financial indicators of investments. For instance, by enhancing houses, enhancing curb appeal, and constructing new housing, responsible real estate investors may significantly influence the neighborhood.

Real estate investors do much more than just get rid of an eyesore when they purchase and renovate a run-down house. Additionally, they make sure that more community members are housed in safe, healthy, clean, and equitable circumstances by providing additional homes for individuals who need them.

Additionally, being a real estate investor needs you to be very active in the neighborhood. Work closely and regularly with lenders, real estate agents, house inspectors, and contractors, hiring them for your possessions additionally, you'll establish connections with locals who may be your neighbors, house sellers, or future tenants. Working with local companies boosts your community's economy and builds a network of experts you can recommend to others.

➢ Numerous Investment Preference

Purchasing a single-family home, a piece of land, or leasing commercial real estate are all examples of real estate investments. The best real estate investment for you will depend on your lifestyle, financial goals, and financial capabilities. You decide what kinds of properties and assets you buy as a real estate investor, as well as how you make money. One feature of real estate that many people find particularly enticing is its flexibility.

The varieties of investment properties you can pick from are listed below.

- Multifamily Properties
- Duplexes, Triplexes, And Fourplexes
- Commercial Properties
- Land
- Vacation Properties
- Apartment Complexes Or Buildings
- Turnkey Investment Properties
- Distressed Properties

Whatever method you use to begin investing in real estate, writing a business plan is crucial. As an illustration, some investors only employ rental revenue to supplement their existing incomes. Others utilize the rental money to pay for costs so they may vacation or increase their investment portfolio. You may clearly assess your strengths and limitations, specify your objectives, and create a strategy to achieve those objectives with the help of a thorough real estate investment business plan.

➢ Effective Ways to Save for Retirement or College Funds.

When done correctly, real estate investing is a reliable method to build wealth over time. Due to this, it is the perfect way to finance a variety of objectives, including retirement and education expenses. For instance, parents may take out a 15-year mortgage to purchase a rental property and deposit the rental money into a savings account. Before the child turns 18, the house might be paid off and either sold or kept as a source of ongoing income.

On the other side, the identical method might be applied to retirement savings or as a supplement to retirement funds. Retirement homeowners may use the cash flow while continuing to increase their equity because rental revenue is extremely reliable.

➢ Fairly Simple to Finance & Build Sovereignty

When compared to other assets, real estate investments are comparatively simple to finance. You may borrow anywhere between 50% and 90% of the purchase price, and interest rates are frequently lower than the projected ROI rate. As you can see in the graphic below, mortgage interest rates are now at 4.73% on average and haven't exceeded 6% in almost 15 years.

In contrast, getting a ROI of 15% or more on investment homes is not unusual. It's vital to realize that the rate of ROI for investment properties can vary greatly, and that there may be other ways to calculate and describe your earnings in addition to ROI. Instead, it is preferable to concentrate on the cap rate or cash-on-cash returns depending on the sort of real estate investment you make. Learn more about ROI, cash-on-cash returns, and cap rates.

Using finance to boost a property's ROI is known as positive leverage, and it is one more financial benefit of investing in real estate. In the stock market, for instance, you would have to invest the following the whole sum of money.

On the other hand, with the correct finance, you may spend $200,000 in a duplex house for only approximately $40,000. You keep the property's profits while the lender contributes 80% of the capital for the investment. Your return on investment (ROI) would be much higher on the real estate investment since the upfront expenditures were so much lower if the $200,000 stock market investment and the $40,000 duplex investment appreciated at the same pace.

➢ Advantages of Investing in Real Estate (Tax)

The revenue generated by real estate sales and rentals is well known. However, there are even more hidden financial real estate perks, such as tax advantages. For instance, depreciation costs for rental property assist owners in dramatically reducing their taxable revenue from the property—and occasionally completely eliminating it.
Other possible tax deductions for rented property include:

- Interest On A Mortgage
- Origination Costs For Loans
- Payments For Insurance
- Utilities
- Upkeep, Fixes, And Enhancements
- Marketing And Advertising
- Fees For Homeowners Associations

- Property Administration

Additionally, there are other methods that enable investors to maximize tax savings, including as Section 1031 of the Internal Revenue Code and Opportunity Zones. When you reinvest your property's earnings in another asset, Section 1031 enables you to defer paying taxes on the sale of your original asset, while opportunity zones let you avoid capital gains by investing in a specific parcel of land. These regulations can be complicated, so it's essential that you fully comprehend how they operate and how they will affect your finances before making any decisions.

➢ Autonomy, Adaptability, And Freedom

There are several personal and non-financial benefits to investing in real estate as a job or side business, but most people just concentrate on the money ones. It enables someone who may or may not have professional training or work experience to amass money and have a significant positive influence on their whole society. Additionally, it offers freedoms that the majority of other professions are unable to, such as financial freedom, time freedom, and the ability to develop your own special company plan.

For instance, investors with a portfolio of properties have the ability to switch their principal residence at any moment for practically no expense. When having a family, many individuals choose a two-story home, however In their elderly years, they choose to downsize to a one-story home since it is easier for them to maintain. As an alternative, you may decide to "house hack," or start off by living in a duplex or triplex apartment to start earning rental money, and then move into a larger home after you have enough properties to meet your bills.

Those with an entrepreneurial spirit find investing particularly tempting because there are so many different ways to do it. You might decide to hold onto property or flip residences in order to allow appreciation generate money. You have the option of owning rental properties and managing them yourself, or you may choose to hire a management company to handle everything. You could even discover that developing property for commercial enterprises or flipping land suits your preferences.

Your options are limitless and unrestricted since you own and control your investing company. For entrepreneurs, this freedom may be tremendously rewarding.
With such a wide variety of advantages of investing in real estate, it's an exciting choice for new investors. It can be tempting to rush into an investment property purchase when an investor is focused on the possibilities, but real estate purchases take time. The most successful investors know how to find investment properties for sale and how to

evaluate them for certain criteria to find the best investment. Although it takes time to learn this process, using the right tools to search for properties is an important step.

ROI FOR RENTAL HOMES IN CITIES

If it is correctly managed, a rental home inside the city borders can be profitable. A leader in turnkey real estate, including property management services, is the JWB firm. The current returns for owned urban homes in the firm network are highlighted in the getting started guide that may be seen directly on this page.

'LOCATION' THE MOST IMPORTANT FACTOR IN REAL ESTATE.

The classic real estate proverb states that "location, location, and location are the only three factors that count in real estate." The truth is that a house with 10 bedrooms, eight bathrooms, soaring ceilings, and a pool adjacent to a trash dump is almost useless.

A little one-bedroom, one-bath house located in the heart of downtown Dallas, on the other hand, would be worth a small fortune. As a result, it is clear that the location is crucial when choosing a piece of real estate to invest in.

What is it about a piece of real estate's location that makes it valuable? Really, the answer is not that difficult. The value is solely determined by the factor of desirability. Desirability is a fluid concept that is very hard to define.

A piece of real estate that is completely unappealing to one person could be the perfect fit for the next person. Additionally, house purchasers, renters, and real estate speculators are all affected by this situation. It holds true for every facet of the real estate industry.

What a real estate investor should prioritize first is their plan for turning a profit on a given asset. The location of the property will determine whether it is in a good or terrible location; purchasing the property is only half of the problem.

An investor could, for instance, decide to purchase a home with the goal of simply watching the market premium real estate is most likely the finest option while looking up. The greatest locations are those close to development or entertainment hubs since there is a significant chance that the property's value will rise just by waiting.

On the other hand, an investor could do better to look at urban homes if his goal is to buy a property with the idea of renting it out and earning a monthly income from it. Urban properties are "prime" rental properties even if they wouldn't be classified as "prime" real estate.

There are also real estate investors that are skilled with a toolbox. Rundown properties can be renovated and repaired by the owners, who can then sell them for far more money than they paid for them and generate a sizable profit. These types of real estate investors frequently find that the greatest locations are in working-class areas with a mix of mid-priced residences.
When choosing a property to invest in, real estate investors take into account a variety of factors. One aspect is what I like to term the "snob factor."

Strangely, buyers will spend far more money for a smaller home in the "correct" area than they will on a larger home in a less desired one. One person's idea of a "nice" neighborhood, however, will not even come close to being the same as another person's.

The "visibility" aspect comes next. If a neighborhood or location has Property prices increase no matter where they are, famous or even notorious. Another aspect to take into account when evaluating how desirable a location for a piece of property is convenience. People do prefer to reside close to their places of employment and their children's schools. Rising gas costs may have a significant positive impact on inner-city real estate values.

For real estate investors, house purchasers, and renters alike, there are a plethora of various elements that might affect how desirable a piece of real estate's location is. The investor will invest if the site is suitable for his objectives.

For the sake of buying a property, the location must be appealing. If the area is ideal for the renter's needs, he or she will rent. In essence, attractiveness may be used to combine all the many elements that go into establishing whether a location is good or terrible.

We are an individualistic country. Each of us has a unique perspective on events. Search the area. Everywhere there are humans who live. They occupy large and small communities as well as urban and rural locations. Who is qualified to define what a "excellent" site actually is?

Beauty is in the beholder's eye, according to a saying. Whatever "floats your boat" means in current parlance. It means "if the location meets your objective, then it's a good location" in terms of real estate.

The value of real estate is significantly influenced by location, as do other factors, such as job rates, the regional economy, crime rates, transit choices, the standard of nearby educational institutions, municipal services, and property taxes.

The medium- to long-term outlook for how the neighborhood is anticipated to change during the investment period is crucial when determining where to locate a property. For instance, the quiet open space behind a house now may one day be transformed into a busy manufacturing plant, lowering its value. Examine the ownership and planned use of the nearby locations where you propose to make your investment in great detail.

Getting in touch with the town hall or other government organizations in charge of zoning and urban planning is one approach to learn more about the possibilities for the area around the property you are contemplating. You may then decide if the long-term planning in the region is advantageous or unfavorable to your own strategy for the property.

Homebuyers will scramble for practically any home that comes the market during a real estate boom. This is fantastic while it lasts, but once the festivities are over, only those who select the greatest areas will be in possession of the most valued real estate that also depreciates at a far slower pace. The location of a residence is primarily what causes this disparity in value.

In real estate, the phrase "location, location, location" is frequently used. It's sound counsel, but most people don't understand what it implies, so that's one drawback.

Real estate that is valuable must be located in those places with little opportunity for growth are often more expensive than homes in locations with lots of space.
Think over the features, facilities, and accessibility of a neighborhood and development strategies.

A lot may be less appealing for resale if it is close to things like major roads.
As a result of land's propensity to appreciate in value, acreage frequently outweighs a home's quality.

EXACTLY WHY IS LOCATION CRUCIAL?

Let's first examine the origins of this specific adage, which states that location, location, and location are the three most crucial considerations when purchasing real estate. Most people base their decision to purchase a property on how much they enjoy the home or apartment, but when you purchase a property, you are also purchasing a piece of land. You can remodel or renovate the house that is already there, but you can't move the house from where it is now. This is especially evident in suburban areas houses, which delineate a property's boundaries.

But even if you purchase an apartment in a metropolis, you are still making an investment there. As with the neighborhood of a house, a city block might be a "good" or "poor" investment. This means that a property's value is frequently influenced by location more than any other factor. The simple law of supply and demand applies here: The number of residences in an area limits the amount of housing that can be built there.

PURCHASERS OF HOMES AND LOCATION

The First is to acknowledge that the likes and preferences of the majority of homebuyers, typically determine what makes up a popular region.
A "excellent" neighborhood for homebuyers often features access to transportation, reputable schools, and active local communities.

The Second crucial point to understand is that a "good" or "poor" location won't remain that way indefinitely. Cities, towns, and even suburban communities go through ongoing change. Within a few years, a neighborhood may go from being less attractive to being seen as "up and coming." For instance, it is frequently worthwhile to purchase in an area if a significant firm just established close by an affordable neighborhood.

LOCATIONAL FACTORS

Of course, what constitutes a desirable location may vary from person to person, but there are other objective elements that affect a home's worth. You might not be able to purchase a home with all the amenities you like or need based on your individual requirements of these elements. That's OK too. A house is after all much more than simply a financial investment.

When you are looking for a property, consider the local amenities. Buyers typically seek out convenient dry cleaners, food outlets, and entertainment. Think about driving on the highway, using the bus, and using public transit like bike-sharing stations and subway stations. The value of a residence will often increase with proximity to amenities.
But have these five things in mind the next time you're looking for a new home.

CENTRALITY

Undoubtedly, where you choose to reside in a city or town will have an impact on your housing costs. Cities like San Francisco, which are heavily developed and don't have a lot of opportunity for further expansion, tend to have a limited supply of land greater costs than cities with excessive expansion potential. Some of these neighborhoods have a large number of vacant homes and run-down regions.
The U.S. Census Bureau reports that population increase is typically to blame for this urban sprawl.

The outlying sections of vast cities typically endure the most significant decreases in property value when a population exodus occurs. This is one way that geography affects the basic economic principle of supply and demand.

Find out whether anything, such as any planned developments, construction, or new home starts, is likely to significantly alter the neighborhood. Despite a site appearing great, it may soon experience significant changes, some of which may be for the better a location's popularity

NEIGHBORHOOD.

The areas that you find appealing will mostly depend on your particular preferences. A genuinely outstanding community will, however, share a few essential characteristics, including facilities, accessibility, and attractiveness. The size of the property on which your house is built may also be determined by your community.

In terms of accessibility, search for a community close to a city's main transport lines that has several entry points. Many individuals spend a significant portion of their days traveling to and from work, so a home that is conveniently located near highways and public transportation will be more appealing than one that is hidden away and has only one route to it. Shady trees, lovely landscaping, and close proximity to public places likely to be favored.

The amount of time houses in a community are on the market indicates how well-liked it is; if sales are moving quickly, you may assume that others agree with you.

A wonderful community should also have necessary facilities like grocers, retailers, and eateries. Most individuals want to go to convenient areas often. Even if you don't have children or don't intend to, do some research on the public schools in the area. A good public school system can increase local property prices and affect the profit you can make when you decide to sell. Additionally, you'll want to draw in as many potential customers as possible. Many purchasers seek for areas with top-notch public schools.

EVOLUTION

Future amenities are equally as important as those that are available now. Plans for additional municipal infrastructure, including public transit, schools, hospitals, and other facilities, can significantly raise local property prices.
Property values might also rise as a result of commercial development. If any new public, commercial, or residential developments are anticipated, attempt to learn about them before starting your search for a property and think about how they could alter the neighborhood's appeal.

Most people desire to live in an area with a low crime rate, which is also a welcoming and safe environment to be outside and mingle with neighbors.

LOT LOCATION

The location of the house must also be taken into account. If the If the house you wish to buy is close to a highway or directly on a busy road, you can definitely purchase it for less money, but it will be more challenging to sell in the future.

The same may be true for homes that are adjacent to or back onto a business building, such a grocery store or petrol station, as well as for homes situated on streets with unusually high parking demand and parked vehicles, including those next to major churches or community centers. As an alternative, a home with a stunning view or close to water is likely to be more valued both today and in the future.

It is forbidden to discriminate in mortgage financing. If you feel that you've been treated unfairly There are actions you can take if someone is harassing you because of your race, religion, sex, marital status, use of public assistance, national origin, handicap, or age. Making a report to the Consumer Financial Protection Bureau and/or the U.S. Department of Housing and Urban Development is one of these steps (HUD).

The House You Buy

People are often surprised by one element of house searching. Consider that you have reduced your options to two houses that are next to one other in a desirable area. One has a vast lot but needs renovations and repairs. The other is in excellent condition but is situated on a property that is just half as large as the fixer-upper. The cost of the two houses is comparable. Which one do you pick? The house that needs work is usually a better investment

Your Home Is A Depreciating Asset, This Is Why.

However, compared to the home, the value of the lot will remain the same or even increase. The larger property would fetch a higher price if you demolished both houses. So, a bigger, better-shaped, or better-located property is preferable to a fancier residence, if you can. The lot cannot be changed, but a less appealing home may always be modified, expanded, or completely replaced.
Should I Purchase a Fixer Upper in a Desirable Area?

If you have the time and resources to make improvements, purchasing a fixer-upper in a well-liked or developing community might be a wise investment.
How can I tell whether I'm buying in a good area?
Indicators of a stable community include well-maintained houses and yards, easy access to facilities, low crime rates, public transit, public schools, and paved roads.

Can I Purchase A Home Without A Realtor?

It's not necessary to hire a realtor to get a house. If you're relocating somewhere new, a reputable local realtor can assist you discover more about the communities. They can also respond to inquiries on communities, schools, and nearby activities. You might be able to avoid this step if you're purchasing a new home in your own neighborhood, but realtors may have insider information of home sales and may be able to bargain on your behalf for a higher sale price. Nevertheless, buying a house without one is still feasible. Just be ready to put in the necessary time and effort into your research, documentation, and negotiations with the seller or the seller's broker.

Location isn't wholly arbitrary; in fact, it's determined by a set of rather constant standards. Make sure the community offers traits that will contribute to your investment appreciating in value over time, such as appealing facilities and outstanding schools, in addition to being desirable to you when you start house hunting.

There are a number of methods that might assist you in choosing a suitable house location. It's crucial to understand that the neighborhood's residents are a great source of information if you're considering moving there or merely purchasing property there. People are eager to give information and ideas when you mention that you are seeking to buy in the region to them in a neighborhood coffee shop.

For the same reason, scheduling viewings with a few local real estate agents even if you don't plan to employ their services, estate agents. They will be able to provide you advice on the most attractive (or the most lucrative) spots in the area because they are specialists that operate in the sector. Naturally, they will also assert that each of their houses is in a terrific location, so be wary of what they say. There is no alternative for study once you've reduced your property or location choice to a few contenders. Run the aforementioned considerations by each property you are thinking about.

Currently, the sector of real estate investing is experiencing a little technology boom. It's getting more and more common to base your investment selections on technology and algorithms. Even while they may be beneficial, they won't matter if you forget the most crucial aspect of investing criteria—location. The overused adage "location, location, location" is something we have all heard. In fact, many people agree that it is the single most significant element of real estate investing.

But since it's been applied so frequently, its significance has begun to wane. The truth is that without a suitable location, even the finest statistics will rapidly lose their significance when purchasers or tenants don't turn up curiosity about the property.

With purchasers, price and location frequently go hand in together. When looking to purchase, consider what is most essential to you. Price is excellent, yes, but location is usually preferable. Everything else in the transaction and involving the property will be determined by it. Your home will be more in demand and have a better chance of fetching a higher asking price if it's situated in a good neighborhood. The attractiveness and demand of a given property won't be nearly as high if it is situated in a declining region. A superior site may cost a little bit more up front, but it will provide you many more lucrative choices down the line.

It is simple to purchase the greatest homes in the best neighborhoods, but investing is more difficult. Your portfolio has to be well-balanced between upside potential and value. Your investment strategy and objectives will be determined by the area in which you invest. You are committing to long-term ownership of the home and all of the labor that renting to college students implies by concentrating on houses close to universities. While investing in houses in less desirable areas may yield higher returns, it will be difficult to find buyers for your property. This lack of demand will eventually pinch you in the form of reduced rentals or a lower price selling price.

In most communities, a short distance might provide an entirely different view. Here, it is crucial to ensure that you are paying for the greatest location and are well informed about the area you are purchasing in. Investigate the area's mill rate, employment rates, and new housing starts to see whether any changes are on the horizon. There are occasions when a region may look perfect only to see significant changes soon. You must be well informed on the area you are purchasing in before making a purchase.

If you're having trouble judging a property, start with the location and go back to the fundamentals. This tested and proven evaluator appears to be straightforward nevertheless it is still the most crucial element in real estate.

In the real estate market, purchasers will compete for almost every home that becomes available. An important thing to think about when purchasing a house is the location. The majority of people have no idea about a certain place, hence it is the realtor's responsibility to educate the customer.

Buying a home this year might be quite advantageous.
You have a lot of options because there are so many residences for sale.
Because interest rates are cheap, you can afford the home of your dreams.
Renting a home is preferable to buying one.

In real estate, location matters. In general, houses in metropolitan regions with little room will be more significant than those in places with plenty of space.
Think regarding the neighborhood's accessibility, aesthetics, facilities, and future plans.
It could be less desirable for resale if it's very accessible to things like major highways and public places.

Real estate frequently outperforms homes in terms of quality because lands appreciate.
Location is an extremely important factor to take into account when buying a house.
The motivation becomes obvious if we take a moment to consider what we are buying when we buy real estate. However, a lot of individuals make the decision to buy a piece of real estate based on how much they enjoy the apartment or home. When you buy a piece of real estate, you are also buying a piece of land. It is possible to remodel, build a new, or even demolish the home that is now located there and turn it into apartment suites. The exact location of the land you own is something you cannot alter.

Most residential dwellings, where a property's limitations are explicitly forth, reflect this fact. Regardless, irrespective of whether you are when you buy a home in a city, you are also making an investment in that area.

This suggests that the most important factor determining a property's value is its location.

Homebuyers will consider location while deciding which house to purchase, among other factors. Everyone aspires to own a house in a nice neighborhood. What then makes a place desirable? Schools, ease of access, safety, and more! One of the greatest methods to assess attractiveness is location, particularly when it comes to the "downtown" region of rapidly expanding cities.

The value of an identical piece of property will be substantially different depending on whether it is in the middle of a large metropolis or a tiny, rural village. The significance of the place is due to this. There are many communities in Charlotte, but due to the area's popularity, properties in Charlotte's greatest areas will appreciate the most.

Highly Developed communities that don't have much available space for further expansion are sometimes obliged to construct "up" rather than "out." places like New York, San Francisco, and even the downtown center of Charlotte. A 2 bedroom, 800 square foot apartment can often cost more than a 5 bedroom, 4,000 square foot mansion due to location.

The school system is one of the elements that many homebuyers take into consideration while making their choice. People who have children or want to have children are understandably worried about the caliber of the school that will educate their child. Due to how crucial they are to purchasers, we have included a feature on our website to assist visitors in finding houses for sale by school district!

Even The effectiveness of the school system will affect the value of a property even for those without children. All around the nation, this is accurate. In contrast, it might not be as significant in a community where retirement or tourism are the main industries. Since it is a holiday house, residences near beaches and secondary homes are often less concerned with school districts.

Everyone want to live in a secure area. Low-crime areas are thought to be more suitable places to live, and as a result, their property prices are greater.

In certain cities, particularly in the core sections, violence can vary noticeably from block to block. You may use online crime statistics and local crime reports to gauge how safe and secure an area is.

Looking at some of the most expensive cities in the nation, it is easy to understand how crime affects property values. Different neighborhoods' property prices in high-cost-of-living cities like San Francisco and New York will range greatly from one another. You will see if you take initiative at the project that locations with a high frequency of crime will be significantly less expensive than those with little to no crime.

Some neighborhoods in cities with crime issues could have gates. Although not every region will provide a gated community choice, living in one is seen as a safer and more secure alternative, and as a result, these properties may command a higher price.

Among the way people travel about the neighborhood and city is one of the reasons location is so crucial in real estate. Shopping, dining, entertainment, and grocery shops may all be easily accessible by foot from certain property sites. Others may offer convenient, secure public transit choices that make it simple for people to move throughout a crowded metropolis. Living in a city with excellent public transit alternatives is viewed as more attractive since you won't need to use your automobile all the time; in fact, some people may not even need a car.

On the other hand, certain urban areas and the majority of rural areas mandate that residents own a car. The amount of traffic in some parts of the country can make commuting and conducting errands difficult longer than they ought to be.
Amenities

Another aspect that affects how appealing a location is its accessibility to facilities. There is a significant difference between needing to drive 45 minutes to get a carton of eggs and being able to rush to the grocery store in five minutes.

In addition to the requirements, upscale luxuries and other opulent services can influence how appealing a place is. A location may be more appealing if it is close to a yoga class, gym, well-known eateries, and shopping centers.

The Importance of Location in Real Estate When Purchasing a Home!

American cities sometimes consist of several distinct neighborhoods, each with its unique traits and qualities, For instance, choosing a family in Los Angeles merely based on the neighborhood they reside in might mean quite different things.

There is little doubt that your own preferences have a role in the communities you find appealing. However, a lot of people will be curious about the neighborhood's features, look, and accessibility. How big your lot is might also be influenced by the sort of area you reside in.

Many individuals choose to reside in areas where they can travel quickly to and from work. This indicates that they are seeking for areas with convenient access to either major roadways or public transportation.

Depending on how they look, various communities might give off very distinct vibes. Houses, with beautiful gardens and big Parks and communal areas with trees are often far more inviting than those without.

It's also quite crucial to consider the local amenities. There is a significant difference between being able to stop at your local grocery shop and needing to go somewhere else. The quality of a neighborhood is also significantly influenced by the local school district and the level of crime.

Potential For Appreciation In The Future

The housing market is not a static thing. Instead, it is always ebbing and flowing. In a decade or two, areas that are currently thought of as unpleasant will certainly be in vogue.

However, certain communities may be starting to experience a fall in appreciation.

Sometimes it isn't what will happen to a neighborhood over the period of years or decades may probably be predicted. However, there are some areas where the correct indicators of future appreciation potential may be found.

The position of a property's location is also influenced by future development plans. Property values in the neighborhood may increase if plans are made for municipal infrastructure such as hospitals, public transit, or new schools. When it comes to commercial development, this is also accurate.

One of the finest new construction house purchasing advices we can provide is to make sure you grasp the future perspective of the neighborhood and region since new construction neighborhoods are probably going to be cropping up everywhere where you reside.

Despite the while the overall location of a home is significant, the location of the particular lot is as significant.

In the same area, not all houses are made equally. Homes built directly on a major road or extremely near to an interstate highway may not pique people's curiosity as much. Similar to this, residences near to businesses or those situated on streets with heavy parking traffic may not be as desirable.

On the other hand, homes that are close to water or have a stunning view are typically more expensive than those without. In the same neighborhood as a house that borders a park, if everything else is the same, property that borders a busy road will likely be worth more.

WHAT OTHER FACTORS AFFECT THE VALUE OF YOUR HOME?

While the location of the property has a significant impact on house value, it is by no means the sole aspect. Let's look at some of the other factors that might affect the value of your house.

Your home's value will be impacted by both the local and national real estate markets, particularly in areas that are severely hit during a recession.

For instance, 2020 has been a roaring seller's market with loan rates at historic lows and home inventory also being fairly low. This occurs as a result of a greater demand than supply, this is more evident in certain locations than others, though, if you examine the local marketplaces in different parts of the nation.

The housing market, on the other hand, was oversupplied during the financial crisis of 2008. This indicates that prices decreased as a result of a supply surplus.

How long it takes to sell your property might also be influenced by market circumstances. Your home will probably be on the market longer if you're selling it in a buyer's market. In contrast, your home is more likely to sell fast if you are selling in a seller's market.

The truth is that your local market and global market might affect your house worth even if it is in the ideal location and in good condition.

Age and condition of the house of course, the house itself has a significant role in the value of your property as well.

A house in immaculate shape will sell for more money than a house in the same neighborhood that requires a lot of maintenance.

The house's age will also be a consideration. Even though they may be well-built and maintained, older homes may be thought of as needing more upkeep and maintenance than your home.

When evaluating your house, potential buyers will also take insurance factors into account. Some houses are situated in locations with a high danger of flooding, therefore owners would be wise to buy supplemental flood insurance. Similar to this, a variety of factors, like the materials used to build the home, might affect how much insurance will cost.

Another the size of your property will be a key factor in determining its market value. A price per square foot is frequently used to determine the general worth of homes. However, there is a broad range in what consumers would spend per square foot.

It’s worth is also based on how much usable space it has. Attics, garages, and unfinished basements are often excluded from this. Living space is the most crucial factor for both appraisers and purchasers.

Bedrooms and baths are often the most highly regarded types of useable space. As a result, you may expect your home to gradually incorporate additional bathrooms and bedrooms.

Home remodeling work might occasionally assist to increase the value of your house. Particularly, this is accurate in homes that are older and have outmoded features. It's crucial to realize that not all updates and upgrades will provide you a profitable return on your investment.

Your local market and the value of your property will determine how much an update reduces its value. A project to renovate a basement, for instance, is typically five times more value in Portland, Oregon, than it is in Atlanta, Georgia.

Remodeling the kitchen or installing a full bathroom can occasionally increase the property value of less costly properties. Updates like adding a pool or replacing wood floors in bigger, more costly houses may be a better investment.

A number of different ways, some of which don't necessarily require big improvements, to raise your home's worth. You may sell your home more quickly and for more money by doing things like improving the curb appeal and painting it.

Real estate location has a huge role in your home's worth and how desirable buyers believe it to be.

If you're thinking about selling your house, you might be curious about its value and the state of the neighborhood real estate market. To get an idea of how much comparable houses are selling for in your neighborhood, it might be a good idea to look at other comparable listings.

HOW TO LOCATE HOT MARKETS FOR INVESTING IN REAL ESTATE.

Real estate investing is not a novel strategy for achieving financial success. It is a well-traveled route, and the reason it is so well-traveled is that it is a really efficient method to generate a lot of money in a short amount of time. To make any significant money, however, in the purchasing and selling of real estate, you must be a forward-thinking individual.

To achieve the goal of buying low and selling high, one must make an educated prediction as to what will occur tomorrow, next week, next year, or in ten years, rather than basing their choices on events that occurred yesterday, last week, last year, or in 10 years.

Consider the area where you were raised. Your parents acquired the home when the community was still a new development. It is no longer novel. It is not moving upward. It is moving downward.

Both the population and the structures are getting older. That is how real estate works. Everything that rises will ultimately fall. Always buy while the region is expanding rather than when it is contracting. Of course, there are exceptions to this rule, but they are few.

In order to acquire investment property, you must locate the hot markets. To put it simply, the hot market is where the people are going. Figuring out where people go is the key.

If you can get a good bargain on the property, buying in a location that is currently popular may be a hot market. However, learning about anticipated infrastructure upgrades might help you predict where people will be moving in the future.

Construction of expansive highways, marinas, or entertainment venues are examples of infrastructure modifications. In essence, you should base your real estate market investments on the facts rather than what you think will occur or what your barber says you.

While it's not the best time to buy real estate in the US right now, you may still benefit greatly from hot properties abroad while you wait for the US real estate market to rebound. Costa Rica is an excellent illustration.

Only three hours separate the mainland from Costa Rica. It is a very well-liked holiday spot, and beachfront property has been increasing in value for a while now, but it looks like the trend will continue.

Investment in real estate is not a precise science. If you do decide to invest in foreign real estate, it is advisable to hire a local attorney to handle the transaction since you must always consider the risk with the possible benefit.

Additionally, when looking for attractive investment real estate, the "cool" element should not be disregarded. For instance, in California, there is a region known as "the Venice Beach" region. A few years ago, a movie was produced there area was packed with skateboarders and surfers a few years ago. Real estate prices in Venice Beach skyrocketed as the area overnight gained a lot of "cool" appeal! Don't ignore "cool," then.

Keep a close eye on big business's expansion intentions. Simply because of the need for homes and small enterprises, the real estate market will grow when corporations create, expand, or even migrate. Can a McDonald's be long behind if a Wal-Mart is being constructed in a town? Additionally, housing will be required for all of the new employees who will be hired to manage Wal-Mart and the associated small companies.

Yes! Business may develop hot homes for investment objectives and drive up real estate values!

Investment decisions should always be based on reliable information. A marina development permit provides unmistakable evidence that a marina will be constructed and that the prices of the nearby properties will increase.

A marina being built is NOT going to happen, despite what your relative told you. It's rumor, so don't place large bets based on it! Real estate investing is a great strategy to achieve a high return, but you to avoid losing your shirt, you really do need to know what you are doing.

In order to increase the value of their investment portfolio, real estate investors who are looking to develop a solid portfolio keep an eye out for hot markets.

If you discover about hot markets after they have already become hot, you may have missed much of the build-up that made them hot.

Real estate investors that are savvy attempt to foresee markets that will heat up before they happen so they may purchase properties ahead of rising valuations. They make money by selling homes in a competitive market.

Knowing your local market inside and out and keeping an eye out for emerging markets are other ways to uncover chances. Find a fixer-upper in a respectable neighborhood. Search in locations that are close to expensive neighborhoods as well.

Be on the lookout for passable soft obstacles, such as a block that is improving close to a block that has previously improved. It is more difficult for an improving neighborhood trend to transcend hard boundaries like a big boulevard, a motorway, or a river.

It goes without saying that you'll want to locate the hidden jewels before everyone else if you're thinking about going into real estate investment, especially if you want to acquire houses to rent out for revenue. Long-term, investing in an area before it becomes popular at a discount and being able to profit from the rise in neighborhood property values can be a terrific way to expand your real estate holdings. But it's not always simple to arrive early. Purchasing in a location that everyone believed to be on the upswing may not work out due to the whims of taste and cool, which may alter overnight.

There are several things to keep an eye out for, and if you have a little knowledge, do some study, and use your intuition, you could just discover yourself seated on the upcoming hot property. And for you to have all the information you want regarding real estate investment.

The idea is basic. Purchase properties at bargain prices that provide rental income that exceeds your mortgage costs. Run the numbers as a first step. Need assistance with that? The calculations in this article from Bigger Pockets are so straightforward that you may do them on a piece of paper. Like with any investment, you need to know what is coming in and what is leaving; it is in the comparison of the two that the deal's profitability is determined. Some investments pay off over the long term, while others pay off right away. The objective is to move as rapidly as possible into a favorable position.

It's crucial to keep in mind that the houses you're purchasing are purchases. You should long-term safeguard them as investments. If you look after them, they will look after you. The largest error we observe novice investors making when attempting to figure out how to invest $1,000 is failing to treat real estate investing as a serious, long-term undertaking. Do not disregard any repairs that the house may require. The longer you wait, the worse these issues develop and the more expensive they can become. You may save money by keeping your home's systems maintained on a regular basis. If you take care of your properties, they will take care of you.

Identifying Hot Real Estate Investment Markets

Playing a basic numbers game in which you search for locations with low sales is the first stage properties that were purchased and sold quickly. They may have been renovated and sold, or someone may be cutting their losses because the location didn't work out. There could be deals there, but it won't be in your best interest to purchase a home you won't be able to rent out in the future.

Listen. What's trendy and what's not is a topic of constant conversation. Observe where your ideal tenant spends their time and pay attention to what they have to say. They'll explain the direction of the trends. For this type of study, social media may be a fantastic resource. See where developers are investing their money by reading the business publications. However, you shouldn't wait until the last minute, so be prepared to act swiftly if you seem to have noticed an increase in interest. Of course, your instincts are also helpful in this situation. Have you ever seen anything that simply appears too wonderful to be true or that just one person seems to be drawn to? Keep in mind that not all investors are successful, and even the largest enterprises can fail.

Look for days on market while studying the sales statistics for a particular location. Is there a sharp decline in trend? When the average days on market begin to decrease, it can be a sign that investors are beginning to snap up homes because something is happening. But use caution, since it could only represent a typical increase in activity. Here, long-term trends can greatly improve your understanding of the situation.

Contrasting over time these short-term patterns might assist you in determining if this is typical or whether there is a problem. Keep in mind that prices tend to rise as days on market decline. You never want to be on the growth side of pricing, so be sure and schedule your entrance properly. Shorter days on market often come before price increases.

Take a look at the marketplace. Each year, businesses spend millions on market research. They don't pick their next place at random, so if you notice progress, you can be sure they appreciate the region. Before they begin construction, find out where the companies will be. Know the preferences of your potential tenant as well. These days, establishments like high-end grocers and coffee cafes are popular.
Look for mom-and-pop artisan coffee shops, Trader Joe's, and Whole Foods. The better you are at seeing activities before others do, the more you will know about the regional business trends.

Become a part of the city. Attend committee meetings, public hearings, and planning sessions; the more you know about what's going on in your community, the better. Pay close attention to any gatherings where the public is given a chance to speak. Gain insight into what is occurring in their local communities by listening to their worries and ideas. Serving their needs and satisfying their desires will put you in a much stronger position. The best talent an investor can have is listening since individuals will usually tell you what they want and need.

At last, your mother was immediately after she advised you to avoid putting all of your eggs in one basket. Real estate investing is a long-term plan, and neighborhood trends can change. While you might wish to buy more than one home in a hot area, you can also look into other investment alternatives like Forex or day trading. There are several online trading platforms available that might aid with your beginnings.

To maximize your transactions, you need also invest adequate time in your research and locate a reputable online broker in the United Kingdom. While there is a nationwide growth in the number of downtown regions, there was a time when they were neglected in favor of the suburbs and suffered so much for it. Spread out your assets so you have a safety net in case one sector doesn't work out or suddenly becomes unattractive. Similar to the stock market, solid planning can help you weather any home market storms that may arise in your area.

To set and accomplish short- and long-term goals, real estate investors must approach their operations with a business-professional mindset. Making a business plan is a smart idea since it helps investors see the broad picture and keeps your attention on the essential objectives rather than on any little obstacles.
Typically, real estate investors are not required to abide by any specific code of ethics. Even though it would be simple to profit from this circumstance, the majority of prosperous real estate investors uphold strong ethical standards. A real estate investor's reputation is likely to be well-known because it includes dealing with people. Effective real estate investors understand that being fair is preferable to trying to get away with as little as possible.

Effective real estate investors get a thorough understanding of the markets they choose, such as concentrating on a certain geographic area and focusing on residential as opposed to commercial buildings. Real estate investors may recognize present situations and make plans for the future by being informed of current trends, such as any changes in consumer purchasing patterns, mortgage rates, and the unemployment rate, to mention a few. As a result, they can anticipate when patterns could alter, which may present chances for the prepared investor.

For investors to succeed, they must create a focus and acquire the depth of information needed. Long-term success depends on taking the time to develop this degree of mastery in a particular field. Investors who have mastered one market can apply the same in-depth strategy to new markets as well. High-end housing, low-income multi-unit housing, or rural farm renovations are a few examples of specialized markets.

A significant percentage of a real estate investor's revenue comes from referrals, thus it is essential that they treat others with respect. This includes coworkers, associates, customers, tenants, and anybody else the investor does business with. Effective real estate investors pay close attention to the little things, take complaints and concerns seriously, and show their company in a favorable and expert light. As a result, those investors get the type of reputation that attracts the interest of additional potential partners.

Both novice and seasoned real estate investors can benefit from the assistance and possibilities offered by a professional network. Investors can challenge and encourage one another in this kind of group, which may be made up of a carefully chosen mentor, business partners, clients, or members of a charity organization. Smart real estate investors are aware of the value of networking since a large part of the real estate investment process is learning via experience.

INTEREST RATES

People frequently agree to pay more for homes when loan rates are low. On the other hand, high interest rates typically result in reduced home costs.

People's capacity to purchase a property may be impacted by both short- and long-term interest rates. People's short-term debt may become more expensive if short-term interest rates increase. This implies that they might not have as much money as they would want to buy a house.

Like any other type of investment instrument, the value of real estate that generates income is significantly impacted by interest rates. This is notably true for the rates on Treasury bills and interbank transactions (T-Bills). Many people mistakenly believe that the current mortgage rate is the only element affecting real estate worth because of their substantial impact on an individual's capacity to acquire residential properties (by raising or reducing the cost of mortgage capital).

Mortgage rates, however, are just one interest-related element that affects how much a house is worth. Interest rates influence capital flows, the availability and demand for money, and investors' necessary rates of return on investment, among other factors. As a result, interest rates influence property prices in many different ways.

Interest rate may influence home price growth in several different ways.

The income technique considers the net cash flow, just like the discounted cash flow analysis done on stock and bond investments.

A property's supply and demand dynamics can be directly impacted by changes in capital flows, as well as the cost of borrowing and mortgage rates.

The calculation of discount or capitalization rates, which are equal to the risk-free rate plus a risk premium, is where interest rates have the most obvious effect on real estate prices.

Foundations of Valuation

The supply and demand for homes, as well as the expense of building new homes, all have an impact on real estate values. However, value is more complicated than that especially when you take into account how property values are impacted by government-influenced interest rates, capital flows, and financing rates. It's critical to have a fundamental grasp of the income approach, the most popular valuation method used by investors, in order to comprehend these dynamics. The income technique is very similar to the discounted cash flow analysis done on equity and bond investments and is offered by commercial property appraisers and underwriters for real-estate backed investments.

Forecasting property revenue, which takes the form of projected lease payments or, in the case of hotels, anticipated occupancy multiplied by the typical cost per room, is the first step in the valuation process. The analyst determines the net operating income (NOI) or cash flow that is left over after all operational expenses by taking into account all property-level costs.

By deducting any related From NOI, we deduct capital expenditures, investment capital for upkeep or repairs, and other non-property-specific charges to arrive at the net cash flow (NCF). Due to the fact that properties typically do not keep cash or have a specified dividend policy, NCF is used to value equity or fixed-income assets in the same way that dividend-paying cash is utilized. The property value is calculated by capitalizing dividends or by discounting the cash flow stream (including any residual value) for a specific investment period.

How Interest Rates Impact Real Estate Prices

Interest rates have a big impact on mortgage rates and financing expenses, which has an impact on costs at the individual property level and, consequently, values. However, competing investments and supply and demand for capital have the biggest an influence on needed rates of return and financial values. The value of all investments has been directly impacted by the Federal Reserve Board's policies as it has shifted its emphasis away from monetary policy and toward regulating interest rates as a method to boost the economy or ward off inflation.

Interbank exchange rates are falling, which lowers the cost of funds and allows more money to enter the system. The availability of cash, on the other hand, declines when rates increase. When it comes to real estate, the variations in interbank lending rates may increase or decrease the available cash for investment. Demand and supply, or the quantity of money available for real estate acquisitions and development, are influenced by the amount of capital and the cost of capital. As an illustration, when capital is scarce Lenders of capital frequently lend at lower percentages of inherent value or farther down the capital stack. As a result, leveraged cash flows and property values are reduced and loans are provided at lower loan-to-value ratios.

The dynamics of supply and demand for a property may also be directly impacted by these changes in capital flows. By supplying additional funding for real estate development and by influencing the population of prospective buyers looking for deals, the cost of capital and the availability of capital have an impact on supply. Together, these two elements influence how much a property is worth.

By supplying extra funding for real estate development, the cost of capital and the availability of capital have an impact on supply.

SPECIAL PRICES

Interest rates' most noticeable effect on real estate values may be seen in when capitalization or discount rates are derived. The capitalization rate may be thought of as the needed dividend rate of an investor, whereas the required total return of an investment is equal to the discount rate. The capitalization rate equals, where the predicted growth in income is or the rise in capital value, and K often stands for the necessary rate of return.

Because each of these rates is equal to the risk-free rate plus a risk premium, they are all affected by current interest rates. The rate on U.S. Treasuries is the risk-free rate for the majority of investors. They are regarded as risk-free since the likelihood of failure is so remote and they are backed by federal government credit.

Because greater-risk investments need to generate a return that is commensurately higher to make up for the increased risk In order to calculate the risk-adjusted returns required on each investment under consideration, investors add a risk premium to the risk-free rate when calculating discount rates and capitalization rates.

The capitalization rate is equal to the risk-free rate plus a risk premium, minus the projected increase in income, since the discount rate is equal to the risk-free rate plus a risk premium. Discount rates will alter with changes in the interest rates that make up them, whereas risk premiums vary as a function of supply and demand, as well as other risk variables in the market. Real estate values decrease when the needed returns on alternatives or rival investments grow; in contrast, real estate prices rise when interest rates decrease.

Concentrate on mortgage rates as they have a direct impact on home values. Use a mortgage calculator to quickly examine current interest rates if you're a prospective homeowner or real estate investor.

However, it's crucial to remember that fluctuating interest rates have an impact on a wide range of real estate issues. Interest rates have an impact on both the demand for investments and the cost of capital in addition to the price of your new property. These money movements have an impact on the supply and demand for real estate, which has an impact on real estate prices.

The returns on alternative investments are likewise impacted by interest rates, and prices fluctuate to reflect the inherent risk associated with real estate investments. These adjustments to the real estate markets needed rates of return also alter during times of credit market instability. Risk premiums broaden when investors anticipate greater rate fluctuation or an increase in risk, which exerts more downward pressure on real estate values.

Another way to look at it is that the owner of Property A has earned a 5% return above inflation. Therefore, the cap rate is directly correlated with the interest rate offered by banks minus anticipated inflation as it is a real rate of interest. Due to the expenses and hazards involved with real estate ownership, real estate often offers a higher real rate of interest than do banks. This cap rate differential exhibits some cyclicality, but over the long run, it tends to remain fairly consistent, demonstrating the stability of real estate as a component of production.

Real and nominal interest rate differentials have also been comparatively low and constant since 1990 due to low and stable inflation. Cap rates follow the movement of both variables. However, economically and statistically, it is real interest rates that drive cap rates.

The monetary turmoil of the 1970s has complicated the historical link between cap rates/yields and actual long-term interest rates in the United Kingdom, and the cyclical pattern in yields1 is extremely obvious (particularly during the recessions of the mid-1970s, the early 1990s and the GFC of 2008). However, the long-term link between yields and real interest rates is evident, and statistical evidence suggests that the two variables have a one-for-one relationship over time, although with a lag.

Between late 2002 (when the data starts) and late 2017 (when the data ends), Japanese all-property cap rates decreased by 210 basis points (bps). This was far more than the nominal rate decline of 100 basis points and matched the decline in real long-term interest rates. In Germany as well, where yields have there is statistical evidence of a 1-

for-1 link with real long-term interest rates, again with a (rather significant) lag, and both have historically been quite stable.

Occasionally, the cap rate spread above real interest rates is wide; other times, it is narrower. This spread often reflects expectations for rent increases, which in turn reflect supply and demand dynamics. Cap rates tend to decrease when there is a high demand for real estate compared to supply. Cap rates typically increase in areas with strong availability, maybe as a result of a spate of recent completions. The availability of loans and other sorts of liquidity, which occasionally vary with the cycle and other times with central bank advice, may also be reflected by cap rates.

CONCLUSION

Investigating and monitoring possible development regions will help you identify hot markets or hot pockets. Become familiar with the trends. One tactic is to purchase the property early when the prices are still cheap, rent it out for a while, and then sell it later when the market starts to heat up.

Consult with your dependable home mortgage specialist if you're looking to buy a new house or are considering refinancing your existing one.

Contrary to the numerous advertising that promise real estate investment is a simple road to wealth, it is a difficult industry that requires skill, strategy, and attention.

Additionally, since the focus of the company is on its clients and employees, investors stand to gain in the long term by conducting business ethically and with respect. While making quick money may be quite straightforward, building a long-term real estate investment firm takes talent, work, and these 10 crucial behaviors.

Real estate is a difficult industry that calls for expertise, skill, organization, networking, and tenacity.
Real estate market knowledge and education are essential, but they frequently require more than simply classroom instruction.
The successful real estate investor understands the dangers, invests in an accountant, seeks assistance, and builds a network.

The laws, rules, jargon, and trends that comprise the foundation of the real estate investor's business must all be kept up to date, just like they are with any other kind of business. Investors that fall behind run the danger of not only losing their firms' momentum but also facing legal repercussions if regulations are disregarded or breached. Successful real estate investors maintain their knowledge and adjust to any governmental or market changes. Additionally, be abreast of legislation in the areas of financing, taxation, and real estate that may have an effect on your company directly or indirectly.

Investors in the stock market are often barraged with warnings about the inherent hazards of investing and the possibility for loss. However, commercials saying the exact opposite—that it is simple to earn money in real estate—are more likely to be seen by real estate investors. Real estate investors that are prudent recognize the dangers, including those related to the law as well as those associated with real estate transactions, and they modify their operations to minimize such risks.

A large amount of a real estate investor's annual costs are taxes. It might be difficult to comprehend current tax legislation, which takes time away from the company at hand.

Wise real estate investors choose a seasoned, reliable accountant to manage the company's records. Compared to the savings that a professional may offer to the company, the fees connected with the accountant may be insignificant.

Real estate includes the land and any enduring features that are tied to it, whether they are created by nature or by humans. These features might include water, trees, minerals, structures, residences, fences, and bridges. One type of real property is real estate. It is distinct from personal property, which includes items like cars, boats, jewels, furniture, and agricultural machinery that aren't anchored to the ground.

An individual who carries out accounting tasks like account analysis, auditing, or financial statement analysis is referred to as a "accountant." Accountants work for accounting firms or the internal accounting divisions of big businesses. They may also establish their own unique procedures. These professions are certified by national professional groups after completing the educational and testing standards set out by their respective states.

A business plan is a written document that specifically outlines how a company—typically a startup—defines its goals and how it will proceed to accomplish them. A business plan outlines a documented strategy for the company's operations, finances, and marketing. Business plans are crucial documents utilized by both the company's internal and external audiences. For instance, a business plan is used to seek funding or attract investment before a firm has built a solid track record. They are also a useful tool for senior teams at firms to stay on track with their goals and communicate about key action items.

It is essential for a real estate investor to have a strong feel of the market and an understanding of how assets are valued. This will enable you to maximize your financial resources. Spend some time considering the properties without becoming attached emotionally. Walking away from a bad transaction is preferable to regretting it later. You will make wise selections if you approach your possibilities with objectivity and analysis. Real estate investors that spread out their sources of revenue, create a budget, take care of your finances, and accurately appraise and study properties to determine which ones are most likely to be profitable. Make use of the expertise and experience of experts to help launch your real estate investing career.

The younger generation is starting to exhibit interest in the real estate market, which is a strong sector with lots of possibilities for financial gain. Nowadays, young adults desire to own homes and work as landlords.

All you have to do is connect house buyers and home sellers so you can earn commissions. Depending on the price of the property sold, commissions might reach the millions or even the hundreds of thousands. Furthermore, you may earn more money without making a significant capital investment the more agreements you get. Additionally, you can get into an equity partnership wherein your partner finances a real estate project and you manage its completion and marketing. Based on the terms of the partnership agreement, returns would be split.

In actuality, many real estate firms participate in partnerships. Some of the properties you see around are owned by partnerships rather than by specific people. You may keep an eye out for eager investors, make a deal, and form a partnership. By doing that, you achieve success more quickly than if you tried to invest on your own.

www.ingramcontent.com/pod-product-compliance
Lightning Source LLC
LaVergne TN
LVHW080549160826
845677LV00018B/1892